GA(

AND B

GW01458028

Yet more puns, one-liners
and dad jokes

Written by Nick Jones
Edited by Ben Corrigan
Illustrations by Tiffany Sheely

Published by Full Media Ltd 2017

ISBN: 978-0-9930794-6-7

ABOUT THE AUTHOR

A proofreader and copywriter by trade, Nick Jones spends a lot of time working with words. But all work and no wordplay would make Nick a dull boy, so to redress the balance, Nick likes to write jokes in his spare time.

He published his first book, the Amazon bestseller *Gagged and Bound*, in 2014. He returned a year later with *Gagged and Bound 2*, and now he's back with the third in the series, *Gagged and Bound 3*, another collection of homemade puns, one-liners and dad jokes as well as more illustrations by US artist Tiffany Sheely.

Nick lives in Cheshire, UK, with his wife, son, daughter, cats, rabbits and fishes.

INTRODUCTION

When I started writing *Gagged and Bound* in April 2014, I had no idea that I'd write a sequel, let alone be here two years later writing a third. But once you start writing jokes it becomes a habit. Every time someone mentions a phrase, you start trying to figure out a way of turning it into a gag. You start looking for puns in every word you read. You'll be in an amusing situation one day, and whereas other people would think, 'I can't wait to tell my friends about this,' you'll be wondering if the situation could work in a joke format. And you'll always be looking at ways of giving everyday observations a surreal twist.

Having said that, after three books it does get harder to come up with new material, so this may be the last joke book I write – for the time being at least. Thank you very much for buying it – I hope you enjoy it!

Gagged and Bound 3 couldn't have happened

without the help of several people. Firstly, I'd like to thank my kids, Lucas and Chloe, for all those times I've had to sit with them in the middle of the night, trying to get them off to sleep. When you're in that situation, you can't play with your phone, you can't read, you can't listen to music other than the lullabies on the baby monitor – so it's a very good time to just sit in silence and think up jokes.

I must also thank my mum. Partly because she's a wonderful, warm, caring person, but also because she was miffed that I mentioned my dad in the other books and not her.

Thanks to Ben Corrigan and Marion Adams for their respective editing and proofreading skills. Thanks also to Tiffany Sheely for her illustrations and to Chris Curley for the cover.

Lastly, thanks to the following for contributing jokes to this book: Andy Barkham, Paul Brown, Dave Collingwood, Ben Corrigan, Robert Fowler, Andy Height, Richard Jones, Lee Matthews and Jim Murphy.

MEDICATION

I dedicate this book to my editor, Ben Corrigan. It's so reassuring having somebody you can count on to spot all the errors in your book that spellcheck would fail to detect.

GAGGED AND BOUND 3

They say you should always open with your strongest material, but I disagree. Which is why I lost my job as a parachute designer.

My local football team played a cup match on a concrete pitch. They won on aggregate.

Why should you never jumble up the word 'asterids'? Because it could spell disaster.

I took part in a tournament where each player took turns feeding a small bird. It was a round robin.

I heard a rumour about a Canadian politician.

9

It wasn't Trudeau.

Why did the girl buy a coffee pot? So it would perk her later.

I'm taking part in a sponsored silence next week. It's going to be difficult to say the least.

The world's heaviest man has spent £2,000 on a 3-metre snakeskin belt. What a waist.

My local barbers have converted their basement into a male grooming salon. First you get your hair cut, then they shave you downstairs.

When is it OK to push a kid around? When

they're in a buggy.

Do career advisers ever advise people to become career advisers?

I've never visited www.kitchen.com. It's a woman's domain.

Question: What's missing from this list: Corn Flakes, Rice Krispies and Cheerios.
Answer: A cereal comma.

What did the farmer say when he got some new scales for his baler? 'Weigh hay!'

Many years ago I was a bread maker. I was young and I kneaded the dough.

If Philip Glass ate a children's meal, would you say he was half full or half empty?

No matter how much I promote my autobiography, nobody ever buys it. It's the story of my life.

Following their success in reducing poverty in a Philippine city, a charity has now set up the same initiative in Kampala. After all, what's good for Digos is good for Uganda.

Why did the sock think it was going to win a prize? Because it had been entered into a drawer.

Motorway chevrons. They're the way forward.

I bought one of those newfangled wallets that have artificial intelligence. These things pay for themselves.

I had a happy childhood, right up until the day I did my first handstand. That was when my world turned upside down.

Those Anonymous hackers have a lot of personal issues. Have you noticed how often they write to agony aunts?

The price of car tyres has increased over the last year. Manufacturers say that it's due to a rise in inflation.

I think I raised the BAR with that joke.

Have you seen that new US cop show where they just check their tyre pressures all the time? It's called *PSI Miami*.

Teacher: Does anyone know what physiology is?
Pupil: Is it the study of soft drinks, Miss?

Being a vet is like being at school. You have to put your hand up.

I'm an after-dinner speaker. My mother taught me never to talk while eating.

A British racing driver recently went to a fancy dress party as a German footballer. It was Button dressed as Lahm.

I read a fascinating article on drugs once. It was boring when I re-read it sober.

A friend of mine came to me in tears, saying he's sick and tired of his apple tree not bearing any fruit. I told him to grow a pear.

What do you get if you cross one Labour leader with two oxygen atoms? Corbyn dioxide.

From 9am till noon, my wife dresses as a schoolboy and says 'Fan-Dabi–Dozi' repeatedly. She's a little Krankie in the morning.

I've decided to sell my treadmill, as it wasn't getting me anywhere.

I just bought a psychic mind-reading device. What will they think of next?

My wife's always focusing on the negatives. She works at a photo developers.

Did you hear about the naughty boy who was just 6 inches tall? He was a handful.

What's the difference between an ostrich and a gangster? An ostrich buries its own head in the sand.

I hate pickpockets. Why can't they appreciate

that other people's valuables are not to be taken lightly?

If you have to pay a nominal fee to do something, does that make it a fee-nominal experience?

I was looking through the new Next directory and all the page numbers were wrong. It was a catalogue of errors.

I wouldn't get out of bed for less than £10,000 a week. I haven't left my bed since I graduated in 1999.

I couldn't figure out how to open a coconut, but I cracked it eventually.

Don't put the cart before the horse, unless you're trying to spell carthorse.

I've just been to buy some manhole covers. Or underpants as most people call them.

My friend is the unluckiest guy in the world. The only thing in his life that has ever gone without a hitch was his wedding day.

I once asked Gordon Ramsay if I could sample the food he was preparing. He gave me an earful.

Why did moths invade the Euro 2016 final? Because they wanted to have a flutter on the football.

Who's made of bread and sings *Because the Night*? Chapatti Smith.

Nobody could've prevented Pudsey winning 2012's *Britain's Got Talent*. It was an act of dog.

I love lamp posts. They're right up my street.

Why do Irish people swear when they drink Magners? Because it causes serious cider fecks.

My grandfather would never take orders from anyone, which is why he lost his job as a waiter.

I was on a dinner date with a woman I'd just met. It was a candlelit dinner, and at one point she went to hand me the salt, and the candle fell and landed on my lap. I caught fire and stood up yelling, but she just sat there. Eventually I managed to take my trousers off. I said to her, 'Why didn't you throw the jug of water over me?' She said, 'Because I don't put out on a first date.'

I've spent the last decade working on a time machine. That's ten years of my life I might get back.

If you don't want your postman looking at your post, don't befriend him on Facebook.

A newspaper wrote a feature on how gangs are running riot in cities up and down the country. There's just no policing some people.

My mother-in-law likes to partake in historical re-enactments. The old battle acts.

I bought my wife some body spray. It was an Impulse purchase.

Mr Smith, a shopkeeper, takes on a new member of staff called Billy. He spends some time training Billy on the till and then leaves him to serve some customers. Everything goes well, and after a few days he decides he can trust young Billy to close the shop on his own. So Mr Smith leaves at 5pm and tells Billy to lock up when his shift finishes at 8pm.

The next morning, Mr Smith comes into work at 7am to open up. He examines the shop and everything seems fine except for one thing: the drawer of the cash register is wide open. He thinks this is a bit odd but decides that Billy must have left it like that by accident, so he doesn't mention it when the young man comes into work.

Later that day, Mr Smith again decides to leave work at 5pm, and gives Billy the responsibility of locking up. The next morning, he comes in at 7am and, lo and behold, he notices the cash register is open again. Thinking this can't be a coincidence, he decides to ask the assistant about it.

Two hours later, Billy enters the shop to start his shift, and Mr Smith takes him to one side and says, 'Billy, I've noticed for the last couple of days that you've been leaving the cash register open when you close the shop each night. Is there a reason for this?'

Billy replies, 'Yes, Mr Smith. There's a sign over there that says, "Open Till 8pm".'

I ran over a cat today. It's okay, I didn't step on it.

Yale make high-quality door security systems, so is Yale University the school of hard locks?

American 1: Ever since we moved to the UK, my wife has a lot of junk in her trunk.
American 2: You mean her butt is a lot bigger?
American 1: No, I mean she does a lot of car boot sales.

When I read an election campaign poster, I don't just have a quick glance. I have a proper gander.

Tommy Hill Figure

Keep losing the end of your snooker cue? Let me give you a tip.

What skincare brand do football fans use? Oil of Olé, Olé, Olé, Olé!

The good thing about imaginary friends is they're always made up for you.

I try to avoid petrol stations. I find the people there self-serving.

I was in a band called Ethernet. We used to gig a bit.

I walked past a busker, and he was singing, 'Red and yellow and pink and green, orange

and purple and blue, I can sing a –'
I said: 'There's no need for such colourful
language.'

I smoked a spliff once and had a really strong
urge to look at The Scream. I had the Edvard
Munchies.

An outbreak of head lice that are resistant to all
known treatments has left everyone scratching
their heads.

My friend is off to buy the world's biggest road
map. I'm interested to see how that unfolds.

A friend of mine committed career suicide. He
deliberately careered off the road and into a
tree.

Why was the knight's holiday ruined? He lost his charger.

I'm off to university to learn how to become a professional darts player. It's a full scholarship including room and board.

I met Frank Lampard once, who claimed that he'd just had sex with a very noisy woman. He said, 'It's not the first time I've scored with a screamer.'

I was never good at Top Trumps. I'm the master of bottom trumps though.

I was walking past a musical instrument shop as it was getting looted, so I decided to take a stand.

Why was the bull's head squidgy? It was a stress bull.

Which primate likes eating digestives? The probiscuits monkey.

I hate it when terrorists put bombs in public toilets. It's bang out of order.

The revelation of Lance Armstrong's extensive drug abuse gave a new meaning to the phrase, 'The winner takes it all.'

Bob: I work as an investment banker. I put the fun in fund manager.
Barry: I work as a fitter. I put the bath in the bathroom.

I'm addicted to sharing a car with a bunch of mates and driving through underground passages. I've got carpool tunnel syndrome.

A friend of mine asked if I'd mind hoovering his house. I said, 'I have one condition.' He said, 'What's that?' I said, 'A dust allergy.'

How does a marmoset's thumb feel about its fingers? It's not opposed to them.

I got arrested for shoplifting yesterday. I was in a music shop and I asked if I could try out a drum kit, and the guy handed me some drumsticks and said, 'Take it away!'

When running a business, it's always good to go the extra mile. Unless you're a taxi company.

What do you get if you cross a rabbit with beer? Bunny hops.

Why is it that when Clark Kent goes in a phone box and puts his underpants over his trousers, he's called a superhero, but when my dad does it, it's called a nervous breakdown?

I met the Invisible Man once. He tried to deny who he was, but I saw straight through him.

What do you get if you cross an arthropod with the Queen's head? A stampede.

This guy said to me he didn't know which direction South East is. I said to him, 'That's down right stupid.'

What time does a jousting match end? When knight falls.

I've got a part-time job writing margins in exercise books. It's just a sideline.

My sister once trashed her entire house when she was on her period. That's what I call an ovary action.

My dad used to say, 'Fight fire with fire', which is why he lost his job as a firefighter.

Our local Chinese restaurant does an 'all you can eat' buffet. There's just loads of prawn crackers – that's all you can eat.

The ten things that most annoy OCD sufferers, in no particular order, would just annoy them even more.

A judge is having a great time at a swingers' party when he's approached by a familiar-looking man. To his horror, the judge realises that it's a psychopath that he sent down for GBH a few years earlier. Feeling awkward, the judge tries to make small talk with him. 'So how are you doing these days? Are you married?' The man, rolling up his sleeves, replies, 'Yes, you're on 'er.'

I've had enough of using spray deodorant. Roll-on next year!

I was on the beach watching a boat sail by, and suddenly I noticed some flares flying up into the sky. Turns out it was a seventies-themed strip party.

My wife has an infectious laugh. She's got the flu.

Why was Atlas always sad? Because the world was against him.

Bob: Brooms are far more effective at cleaning floors than just using a dustpan and brush. Barry: That's a sweeping statement.

Why do ladybirds enjoy spring? Because they get to go on annual leaves.

33

My first attempt at making my own beer tasted horrible. It was a rough draught.

I hate bacteria. It makes me sick.

What do taxidermists stuff parrots with? Polly filler.

John Humphrys: Your name is?

Contestant: Alexander Thompson.

John Humphrys: Your occupation?

Contestant: Ear, Nose and Throat Specialist.

John Humphrys: And your specialist subject?

Contestant: The ear, nose and throat of Van Gogh.

Do you like playing Who Am I? You need your head read.

I made a joke about my wife's cooking and she got all defensive. I said, 'Sorry love, that was poor taste.'

I got in a row with some friends when we went to the theatre. The front row, to be precise.

What should you do if you find Rainman in your loft? Dust him off, man.

Bob: What's the raciest, sauciest thing you've done?
Barry: I once ran a marathon dressed as a bottle of ketchup.

I bought my wife a romance novel for her birthday, but she said she would've liked something more edgy. So I took it back and got her a Rubik's cube.

Another year she asked for some earrings, so I got her a pair of dangly ones. She said they were too heavy and asked for a lighter set instead, so I bought her a pack of Zippos.

My girlfriend told me she needed more space. So I bought her an external hard drive.

A man goes to see the doctor and the doctor says, 'What's your name?' The man says, 'Emile.' The doctor says, 'Yes, I know that, but what's your name?'

My friend said that she really likes men in caps, so I sent her a sign that said MEN.

I went to the theatre last night to watch *Dracula*. I was out for the Count.

I went to an estate agent to ask about a house. I said, 'Is it overlooked?' He said, 'Yes, you're the first person to enquire about it.'

I have a fear of fat, balding, yellow men. It's called Homerphobia.

When I die I want my tombstone to read: 'Thank you, pall-bearers. Without you I wouldn't be where I am today.'

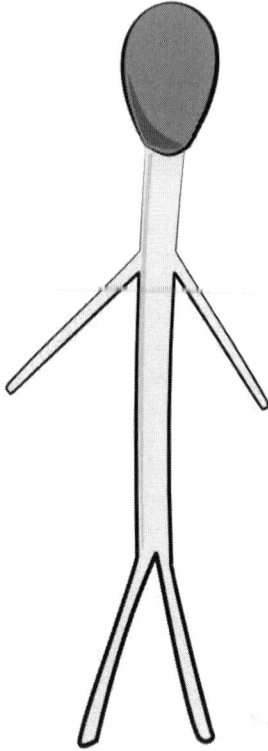

Man of the match

Last year my brother and I both had to endure custody battles over our sons. That separated the men from the boys.

People say I'm outspoken, and it's true, I am. By my wife.

I did something you should never do while driving. I crashed my car.

I like to be firm but fair, so I've just ordered a large bottle of hairspray and some blond hair dye.

What happened to the estate agent when his wife caught him in bed with another woman? He ended up with a semi detached.

I used to work with this woman who always talked about her 'long suffering husband'. Turned out she'd been keeping him on a rack in her basement for years.

I went to the doctor with a headache and asked for something to take the edge off. He gave me a chisel.

I turned on a sixpence earlier. I showed it a photo of another sixpence wearing skimpy underwear.

Dogs bare their teeth when they see someone they don't like, which makes life easy for veterinary dentists.

What's the first thing wasps do when they

build a nest in your loft? They have a house-swarming party.

Why did Rory McIlroy confess to being a naturist on the eve of a major golf tournament? He wanted to get it out in the Open.

I love women, plain and simple. That's why I married my wife.

Countries can be referred to using a two-letter shortcode, e.g. Egypt.

My employer has a strong customer focus. I work for a steroid manufacturer.

What time do boat weddings take place?

Maritime.

Bob: My aunt died last week, so I've just been down to Camden to help clear out her shop.
Barry: Haverstock?
Bob: No, I gave it to charity.

Did you hear about the time Jamie Vardy painted his lounge white? It was a clinical finish.

Why shouldn't you ask Heston Blumenthal to castrate a bull? Because he'll make a meal of it.

What injury did the lawyer suffer? A torn knee.

Whenever I feel down, I call for a taxi. It's a great pick-me-up.

Bob: I've just applied for a job in field sales.
Barry: That's good. What company is it for?
Bob: Sellafield.

I work for a company that manufactures floating beams designed to contain oil spills. Business is booming.

Why was the gemstone happy on its own? Because it was in the pendant.

My radio-controlled clown car has stopped working. It's not remotely funny anymore.

Why couldn't the alcoholic footballer score a goal? Because he kept hitting the bar.

How does God practise safe sex? He uses the Immaculate Contraception.

I'm 38, but I have the body of a 20-year-old. And I'm not going to tell the police where it is.

I just read an article about the alimentary canal. It was an intestine read.

At the school I went to, the teachers were even-handed with the pupils. They hit us with both hands.

What's the best fabric for upholstering chairs? Satin.

Bob: Is it true you have a thing for fat girls who swing both ways?
Barry: Yes, bi and large.

Why is Derren Brown indecisive? Because he's into minds.

Iceman. Butter wouldn't melt in his mouth.

I was in the bathroom waiting for my Viagra

pill to take effect, when my wife called out to me, 'Are you going to be much longer?' I said, 'Yes, that's the idea.'

What's round and chocolatey for no reason? A Revel without a cause.

Once a month, my friends and I get together and dress up as lettuces. We love a bit of cosplay.

Why did the two businessmen go into a guitar shop? They wanted to touch bass.

Why is it that when you mention a film you want to see, people say, 'That's meant to be good'? Surely all films are meant to be good?

Bob: I've just heard that the council are going to plant loads of large trees all over our estate.

Barry: Poplar?

Bob: No, everyone hates the idea.

I think everyone should talk like cats. Come on, hear miaowt.

Why was the wall surrounded by beautiful women? Because it was a stud wall.

My wife sent me to the shop to get some cling film. She was upset when I came home with *Cliffhanger* on DVD.

Where do insects take their used plastic? To the recycling plant.

When a friend of mine lost custody of his son, my wife told me to treat him with kid gloves. So I gave him a pair of mittens as a present.

My company organises marathons aimed at mums, dads and their kids. It's a family run business.

My wife thinks my obsession with computer keyboards is becoming a problem, but I keep telling her it's fine, I've got it under Ctrl.

I went to a drive-in cinema in Italy, but it was so hot I sat on the bonnet. I was on the edge of my Seat.

I did some DIY this afternoon with my new screwdriver. That turned a few heads.

Bob: I was planning on adopting an African elephant and then letting it live in my loft.
Barry: Really? What happened?
Bob: It fell through.

Did you hear about the double act who framed a man for murder, and then ran him over? One set him up, the other knocked him down.

What did the miserable scooter do? It moped.

I went into a clothes shop and asked if I could try on a shirt. The assistant asked, 'Are you a medium?' I said, 'No, I'm a proofreader.'

I'd give my right arm to be ambidextrous.

Apparently The Energizer Bunnies have a new album out. I didn't know they were still going.

I saw two foetuses kissing in public so I told them to get a womb.

In the seventies, this flamboyant-looking man came up to me with a ring binder. I asked him what was in it, and opened the binder to reveal a small piano inside, which he started playing. It was Lever Archy.

I've started doing stand-up routines at prisons around the country. It's nice to have a captive audience.

Take a minus sign and turn it into a plus. OK, you've crossed the line now.

I used to think the grass was always greener on the other side, until I pulled a piece of turf up in my garden.

Bob: Do you have anything on next weekend?
Barry: No. I'm visiting a nudist colony.

It took me a while to figure out how to play Tetris, but eventually everything started falling into place.

I work for a tea manufacturer, but we only make traditional tea, none of that newfangled herbal stuff. I'm a proper tea developer.

Why was the Cyclops good at interior decorating? He had an eye for it.

I spilt apple crumble across the manuscript of my soon-to-be-published novel. The pudding is in the proof.

When I told people I was doing a marathon, they all thought I didn't stand a chance, but I walked it.

My cousin works tirelessly. He drives a tank in the army.

What's made of ice crystals and lives in your stomach? The abdominal snowman.

If you have a high sperm count, it means you're great in the sac.

What's the most negative animal in the world? Horses, because they're all neigh sayers.

I never liked Roy Castle. He was always blowing his own trumpet.

I think I'm in love with chrysalises. They give me butterflies.

Did you hear that Ali G has moved to a Welsh town where he's hoping to become Mayor? For Rhyl.

I had the idea of keeping a fly as a pet but that flew out of the window.

Escalators. They really get me down.

I'm learning how to make earrings out of tiny engines. I'm doing an engine-earring degree.

Did you hear about the woman who gave birth to a 20lb baby? That's no small feet.

Why were French audiences confused when they watched *Jaws*? Because they usually see a Fin at the end.

To de-stress I like to bang my head against a wall. It helps me to forget my problems.

Why is it difficult to disembowel someone? Because it takes guts.

My long-distance girlfriend told me she had a

fetish for polystyrene, so I sent her packing.

The wheels on the bus go round and round, round and round, round and round. The wipers on the bus go swish swish swish, swish swish swish, swish swish swish. The horn on the bus goes beep beep beep, beep beep beep, beep beep beep. I'm pleased to inform you that's a full pass on your MOT.

Did you hear about the time Bono had a nosebleed while eating an ice cream dessert? Sundae bloody sundae.

Bob: Someone just lent me the new Mumford & Sons album.
Barry: Great – let's burn it.
Bob: You mean rip it?

Barry: No, I mean burn it.

Ken Loach has remade the famous Robert Redford and Demi Moore film; in his version, the man offers his old washing machine in exchange for a night of passion. It's called *Indesit Proposal*.

The labour party

That film *Dumbo* creeps me out. It's so eary.

When someone wins *Big Brother*, do they get a reality cheque?

Why did the life coach tell his client to lie face-up on a railway line? Because he wanted to get her back on track.

Why did the casino owner get on well with the brothel owner? They enjoyed each other's company.

How does a magician pull a rabbit out of a hat? It's a trick question.

My pet dog is more intelligent than my pet

parrot, which is saying something.

What does arthritis have in common with an unruly gatecrasher? They both wreck the joint.

If you're not happy with your current sleeping pattern, buy a new duvet cover.

I asked a friend, 'What's the science of projectiles and firearms called?' and he went 'Ballistics'.

Life for an enzyme must be hard – never getting to see the outside of a cell.

I was in the gym, lifting a barbell, when I got cramp and couldn't move. Luckily someone came to assist me. That was a huge weight off my shoulders.

Why did the baby refuse to get in her crib? It was a boy cot.

My wife hates it when I say Grace at the dinner table, which is understandable as her name's Claire.

Andy Murray has never beaten Rafael Nadal on grass, which is why he should probably stop smoking cannabis before matches.

I spent all day shovelling material into a hole in my garden. It was hardcore.

Microsoft have announced that the new version of Word will only have two alignments: left align and centre. How do you justify that?

How does a sniper get rid of his zits? He picks them off one at a time.

I fell in some stinging nettles last week and have been feeling down ever since. I think it might be post-nettle depression.

Patient: Doctor, I keep thinking I'm a hurdle. Doctor: You really need to get over yourself.

I've started playing rock-paper-scissors for cash. I'm making money hand over fist.

Apparently all the toilets in Aretha Franklin's house flush automatically. Cisterns are doing it for themselves.

Why are cemetery workers annoying? They're always having a dig.

Why did the lonely scientist clone himself multiple times? He wanted to make people like him.

My sister fancies rugby players. She thinks they're scrummy.

I remember when the wife and I used to have sex in our pet's hutch. We were at it like rabbits in those days.

Why did the circus's accountant want to see the tightrope walker? He was looking for an outstanding balance.

When doing work experience, it's always wise to take notes – unless you're in a bank.

Why did the burglar put his spliff in a box? He was casing the joint.

I enjoy doing the cancan. Just for kicks.

Did you hear about the incontinent sous-chef? He was always chopping and changing.

Why was the vomit naughty? It was just the way it was brought up.

Have you heard about the pathologist who does post-mortems standing on his head? He's autopsy turvy.

I hate it when people talk during a film, so now I only watch silent movies.

My grandad learnt his trade through trial and error, which is why he lost his job as a judge.

Patient: Doctor, those Viagra pills didn't work.
Doctor: Sorry about that. No hard feelings, eh?

I'm down with the kids. Our pet goldfish just died.

What did Nick Park say to the plasticine? 'I'll

make a man out of you.'

I was running the barbecue at a celebrity party one hot summer's day, when James Corden came over and said, 'Can you throw some more on?' So I picked up Katie Hopkins and launched her into the air.

Glass coffins. I would be seen dead in one of those.

What's the best way to watch *Ghostbusters*? On an ectoplasma TV.

I was parking my car when I noticed a traffic warden by my window. I wound the window down and he shouted very angrily, 'You can't park here!' I shouted back at him, 'Why not?

There are no yellow lines, no parking notices and no traffic cones, so why can't I park here?' The traffic warden replied, 'Because you're on my foot!'

My wife discovered my mistress's fake boob implant in my bottom drawer. I told her I like to keep a breast of current affairs.

Which Jedi Knight is good at getting rid of headaches? Anadin Skywalker.

Teacher: Can anyone give me an example of foul play?
Pupil: *Mother Goose*?

Bob: If you took a penalty with David De Gea in goal, do you think he'd be able to save it?

Barry: I wouldn't put it past him.

My friend is always spitting his dummy out. His ventriloquism act is the weirdest you'll ever see.

I just got a vasectomy via BUPA. It was a snip at £300.

I've lost my calculator a countless number of times.

Men hate washing clothes. That's why washing powders are called 'detergents'.

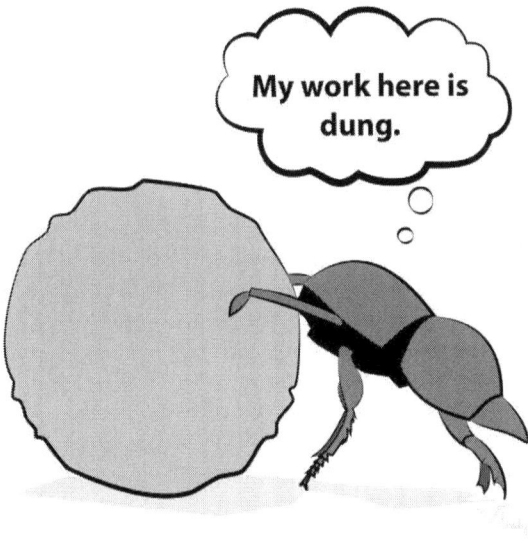

I lost my job at a calendar manufacturer. All I did was take a few days off.

My friend lost an arm in an accident and has been in a coma ever since. He doesn't know what he's missing.

A great name for a cover artist: Vanessa Parody.

Why are door manufacturers always noticeable at parties? Because they know how to make an entrance.

What is Jewish people's favourite cut of beef? Rabbi steak.

Waiter: Would you like water with your meal?

Customer: Yes, please.

Waiter: Still?

Customer: Yes, I haven't changed my mind.

How did seventeenth-century Europeans get their vitamins? They drank Baroqua.

I took a girl on a date on Bonfire Night but we arrived late. We got on well, but there were no fireworks.

I once made my wife eat a two-headed pony. I thought she'd asked me to take her for a freak horse meal.

I was in the pub last night with some friends when one of them started crying. He said he was pretty sure his girlfriend had been sleeping around. To make him feel better, I said, 'Don't worry, mate, we've all been there.'

Have you seen that new film *Dead Leg*? It's a sensation.

What do you get if you cross a zebra with an invisible cloak? Hit by a car.

I got stage fright trying to go to the toilet. Not surprising, really, with 5,000 people watching me.

I got an F in my Maths exam so I appealed. When it came back, they'd given me a U. It was a degrading experience.

How did Quasimodo know that he was unattractive? He had a hunch.

I like pyramids up to a point.

Bob: I just ate some fruit cake from the German market.
Barry: Stollen?
Bob: No, I paid for it.

I used to like my friend Pete, but since he's started taking cocaine and steroids, he's become so high and mighty.

I didn't know where on my body the septum was – but there it was, under my nose the whole time.

I can't stop doing dot-to-dot books. I've never known where to draw the line.

Sixty per cent of people who walk over hot coals are conscious of their carbon footprint.

Why didn't the man go to the funeral at 10am? He wasn't a mourning person.

I asked my wife if she found me more attractive with or without glasses. She replied, 'You definitely look more attractive when I'm not wearing glasses.'

Why do some exit signs include a picture of a stickman? Go figure.

I did a self-portrait in art class, but the teacher was not impressed. She said I needed to take a long, hard look at myself.

What do I know about the number one? Next to nothing.

Why did the actor have a sideline business making crash mats? Because it's good to have something to fall back on.

Did you hear about the man who was hit in the face with a hatchet, losing all his teeth? Police are saying it was axe-a-dental.

Why did the airport close down? Too many overheads.

Why didn't the bicycle want to go out? Because it was two-tyred.

My job requires complete concentration. I work in an orange squash factory.

What does a monk call his private parts? The never regions.

Apparently it costs £6,000 to climb Mount Everest, which is very steep indeed.

Did you hear about the man who balanced tiny sweets on the end of his feet? He thought that was how you play tic-tac-toe.

Why are bus drivers down to earth? Because

they never forget their routes.

Why did the soldier pour a tin of paint over his head? He wanted to be the most decorated serviceman in history.

Why did the chess player organise a tournament on top of a multi-storey car park? Because he wanted to compete at the highest level.

I've just heard that vandals have burnt our local library to the ground. There are no words.

I visited the wreckage today and there was an eerie silence. I thought, 'At least it hasn't changed in that respect.'

I played naked Twister with some friends and ended up getting thrown out of the theme park.

My grandad would always lose his rag, which is why he failed as a window cleaner.

What type of fire relaxes babies? A pacifier.

Why aren't the sides of a football pitch equilateral? Because if they were, the game would always end all square.

People often say I'm mad living on top of a mountain. I can see where they're coming from.

My wife always has to have the last word, which makes Scrabble complicated.

I used to go to the zoo as a child, until they finally realised I was an adult.

Surely everyone's always under the weather?

If I could find a cure for cowardice, I'd bottle it.

Forward Slash

Bob: Did you know that the world's fastest man can reach similar speeds to that of a young horse?

Barry: Usain Bolt?

Bob: No, I'm saying colt.

Why was the magician's table fed up? Because people were always playing tricks on it.

Last night I got drunk and put a whoopee cushion under my pillow. I surprise myself sometimes.

I once rang in sick for work while out shopping, only to realise that my boss was in the same shop on his mobile. It was a close call.

Bob: My friend's wife was so sick of him

playing computer games, she put superglue on his joypad.

Barry: Oh dear, how's he doing now?

Bob: He's holding up.

Some homeless people believe they can get by through selling *The Big Issue*. I beg to differ.

Apparently Simply Red's singer has been kidnapped from their tour bus. That's just taking the Mick.

On weekends, I marry couples at my local church. It's my altar ego.

I love the logo on the back of my tablet. It's the apple of my iPad.

My friend told me she's thinking of splitting up with Dave Grohl. I think she's off her rocker.

Scientists have invented a lotion that can almost instantly cure sunburn. Just let that sink in for a minute.

You can always trust meerkats to give you a heads-up.

Why should you never tell a mole any news? Because they like to be kept in the dark.

Ronnie O'Sullivan has refused to accept responsibility for his recent spate of thefts. He told the police, 'I've been taking cues from someone else.'

My chiropractor has a glossy brochure containing pictures of all the spines he's healed. He's very proud of his back catalogue.

Did you hear about the cannibal surgeon? His patients went under the knife and fork.

What do you call a trainspotter with an eating disorder? Anoraksick.

I've created a typeface called Omniscience. It's the font of all knowledge.

How does Coolio play backgammon? With a gangster's pair of dice.

Have you heard about the guy who steals from

his own grandmother to fund his cocaine, amphetamine and caffeine addiction? I don't know how he sleeps at night.

Buying a new TV these days is so complicated. It's never black and white.

I'm reading a book called *100 Things To Do Before You Die*. The first one is write a will.

I went to a trophy shop and said I was organising a run for charity. The shopkeeper shouted, 'What do you want, a medal?' I said, 'Yes.'

I asked Peter Jackson if I could appear as an extra in *Lord of the Rings*. He said, 'No, sorry,' and then screwed his face up like Gollum. It was a Tolkien gesture.

My brother has finally agreed to donate his kidney to me. I knew he had it in him.

Why would Real Madrid make good post office robbers? Because their counter attacks are dangerous.

Where do fish get their cash? From the hole in the walrus.

My TV is made of parchment. It's paper view.

Abbey Road is The Beatles' crossover album.

Would you like an Asian marriage? That can be arranged.

I make loads of money in my job. I work for The Royal Mint.

Have you seen that film *Hairdresser*? She dyes at the end.

Kleptomaniac clowns. They don't take anything seriously.

Why does Zane Low always carry a chickpea with him? He likes to keep his finger on the pulse.

In hospitals, why do they call the room in

which surgeons operate a theatre? Because it's a play on wards.

Patient: Doctor, I can't stop thinking about the main character from the US show *Breaking Bad*. Doctor: Sounds like you have Walter on the brain.

I was watching a TV show about sailing and they kept saying 'seaward'. I thought people were offended by the seaward?

A lorry load of Vicks VapoRub was spilt over the M6 today. There was no congestion.

Did you hear about China's biggest ever dumpling? It was one ton.

I saw my cat eating a mouse while it was still moving, so I broadcast it on YouTube. It was a live feed.

My friend got a facelift from a budget plastic surgeon. She hasn't stopped smiling since.

Why did the chicken cross Torode?

My friend Colin isn't the sharpest tool in the box. Last year he got arrested for shoplifting, and I advised him that, to avoid implicating himself in court, he should answer the judge's questions with another question. On the day of the trial, the judge started by saying, 'Mr Smith. Did you steal clothes from the shop?' And Colin replied, 'Your honour, is the Pope a Catholic?'

To be successful on Twitter you must have the following.

My daughter thought her new dress was boring, so I cut decorative features into it. She was frilled.

When he's alone in his house, my friend

Laurence dresses up as a woman. He's a Lauren to himself.

Bob: My psychiatrist keeps telling me I need to open up.
Barry: Yeah, my dentist says that to me too.

I've been suffering from amnesia for as long as I can remember.

Bob: I think this cloning machine is great.
Barry: That makes two of us.

What do culinary arts students write at the end of their degree? A dessertation.

Did you hear about the man who fell in a

cement mixer? He was mortarfied.

Where do dermatologists hang their baubles? On the eczemas tree.

I'm very good at making little beach seats for dried grapes. You could say it's my raisin deckchair.

Whenever I'm at a buffet, I let my elders go first. I take after my dad.

The Scouts. They teach you what knot to do.

A pair of tiny beetles were in my garden, so I stood on the smallest one. It was the lesser of two weevils.

I went to a rave on Fireworks Night. The music was banging.

An obnoxious robot just came up to me and extracted all the sodium out of my body! I've never been so unsalted.

Teacher: Can anyone give me a sentence using 'additional'?
Pupil: Yes, sir. 'Give me some food, please, and I need a dish 'n' all.'

People with no sense of direction make terrible films.

What did the detective do when he suspected his daughter had nits in her hair? He combed the area.

Why do ornithologists recommend a gluten-free diet for certain bird species? Because they want to separate the wheat from the chaffinch.

My new chiropodist can't tell her left from her right. So we got off on the wrong foot.

Charlie's mum was not happy that her academically smart son didn't get an A on his latest essay. He was B rated.

It worries me that my son doesn't like trains anymore. He's really gone off the rails.

A leading shampoo manufacturer has launched a new product for people who have hair in unusual places. It's called Head and Shoulders Knees and Toes.

Some experiences are weird at the time, but you can laugh afterwards, such as inhaling nitrous oxide.

Whenever a friend comes round to play FIFA, I make them sit on the floor while I relax in the leather armchair. I always win comfortably.

My business adviser said that I would never get a licence for my Scottish fish farm, because I couldn't decide on a breed. But I told him it was a Dundee eel.

Never in a million years did I think it would be possible to live this long.

Whenever I win anything at a tombola or a raffle, I put it in a display cabinet above the fireplace in the drawing room. It's where I keep my prize possessions.

I saw a horseshoe and thought of U.

You ain't seen nothing until you've closed your eyes for the first time.

They say that men think with their penises, and a small part of me agrees with that.

I'd like to thank my gender reassignment specialist for making me the man I am today.

Why did the comedian take a mohair blanket on stage? He wanted to try out some new material.

When someone's described as a diamond geezer, it means they have a jewel personality.

My mate's a vegetarian. It's not because he cares about animals; he just really hates plants.

Never seen a Matt Damon movie? You don't know your Bourne.

Why did the company run by vampires go bust? Because they didn't want any stakeholders.

Nicholas Nickelback

I bought myself a soprano singer. She's top of the range.

Why were people surprised when a grape won Wimbledon? Because it was unseeded.

Bob: I just bought my wife a long cloth garment from India.

Barry: Saree?

Bob: I said I just bought my wife a long cloth garment from India.

My dad was a late developer, which is why he got fired from Jessops.

What's the best way to attract a Smurf? Talk to them till you're blue in the face.

NASA have announced that they will be launching a lion into space. You can imagine the uproar.

My friend wanted to buy a new TV and asked me for advice. I said, 'For what it's worth, I always look at the price tag.'

Why did the man buy a heated ladder before his holiday? He wanted to set off for warmer climbs.

People go on about how beautiful Mona Lisa is, but she's no oil painting if you ask me.

When I was typing an Italy travel guide, I decided to change the font to italics. Well, you know what they say: when in roman.

I was going to go sightseeing today, but it was too foggy. It was a mist opportunity.

What did George Formby sing when he ran his antivirus software? 'When I'm cleaning Windows'.

Bob: Why have you given me a radiator? Barry: It's a house-warming present.

After 20 years of trying, I still can't pass my English GCSE. Words fail me.

Have you heard about the farmer who plans to create clones of his male sheep? Experts are worried about the ramifications.

On my first day in my new job, my colleague took me to the Managing Director's office. That showed me who's boss.

In my art class, the teacher assigned each pupil a piece of bedroom furniture to sketch. I drew the shorts drawer.

I was bullied a lot at school. One time, the kids snatched my favourite book off me and filled in pages 33–45 with a black marker. That was a dark chapter for me.

I think I'm allergic to treadmills. I went on one and it gave me the runs.

He who laughs last took the longest to get the joke.

My new joke book is ready to publish! I sent the draft to my editor, and the next day he got back to me and told me it's in a complete state.

Minutemen bassist Mike Watt has released an album of Brian Eno covers. It's called *Watt Does Eno*.

Colonic irrigation is expensive. I had a treatment the other day and they cleaned me out.

I auditioned for *Dragons' Den* with my idea for a paper tent, but it was too hard to pitch.

Bob: I'm thinking of selling my sports car.
Barry: Oh really, what year?
Bob: This year.

When buying a calculator, I don't care what it looks like. It's what's inside that counts.

I don't like Barry Gibb. He gives me the 'he be Bee Gees'.

Teacher: Can anyone tell me what is meant by 'Under starter's orders'?
Pupil: Is it where a waiter writes the mains orders, Miss?

Bob: I went to watch the Scottish play last night.
Barry: *Macbeth*?
Bob: No, Celtic versus Rangers.

I told a vampire to look in a mirror. He said, 'I can't see myself doing that.'

Bob: I've just been to a town in Hampshire.
Barry: Havant?
Bob: Yeah I have.

What did Cuba Gooding Jr say when he visited Tutankhamun's tomb? 'Show me the mummy!'

When is a party conscious? When it's a wake.

I showed my two-year-old son how to kick a football. It didn't take him long to pick it up.

I just rang work and told them I can't come in because I've fallen in cement. That's my excuse and I'm sticking to it.

Every night I have sex with my wife in the

missionary position. She wouldn't have it any other way.

A UK rapper has brought out his own range of guitar cables. It's called Leads By Example.

Why are couriers insecure? Because they always take things personally.

Did you hear about the human cannonball who broke his spine? He really landed on his feet.

Why did the Ghostbusters' hiking trip take forever? Because they didn't want to cross the streams.

What's the best way to torture a graduate?

Mortar boarding.

What's the difference between Prince Charles and a bridal bouquet? One's heir to the throne, and the other's thrown into the air.

Did you hear about the drug baron who sold his yacht and bought a barge? He's on the straight and narrow now.

A man appeared in court today for hanging a banner across a bridge that read, 'Say no to fracking'. Believing that the punishment should fit the crime, the judge gave him a suspended sentence.

When I was a kid, my grandad used to let me cover him in fuzzy felt. He was a soft touch.

If you have a weak bladder, urine trouble.

When Mick Jagger dies, will his kids release a cover of *Papa Was a Rolling Stone*?

If you've got an IQ score of 150, you're playing Scrabble wrong.

I was disappointed by the Tetris movie. I think they built it up too much.

Why did Rowntrees bring out an Obama-shaped jelly? Because they wanted to set a president.

Have you heard about the website that can detect arthritis in rodents? All with just a few clicks of the mouse.

I recently splashed out on a new carpet. So now I have laminate flooring around the toilet.

People with limp handshakes need to get a grip.

People who don't finish sentences off properly are idiots. End of.

Hasbro have brought out a dice game for fascists. It's called Nahtzee.

Bob: I've seen a car on eBay for a really low price.
Barry: Oh yeah? What's it on for?

Bob: Because the guy wants to sell it.

I don't like dragons. They're too lairy.

A dad catches his son reading a pornographic magazine. He says, 'What are you up to?' And his son says, 'Page 24.'

My dad always says that you never get anywhere by standing still. He didn't last long as a street statue.

Bob: I badly injured my shoulder the other day.
Barry: Dislocation?
Bob: No, over there.

Cosmetic surgery. Taking old people back to the middle ages.

I just found out that in his youth, my grandfather was a librarian, a mime artist and then a Cistercian monk. He kept that quiet.

Bob: Is that your new pet? It's really small.
Barry: Yes, it's my newt.

What's unusual about Miley Cyrus's computer? She has a TWERKY keyboard.

Why doesn't Donald Trump ever take responsibility for his career failures? Because a bad tool always blames his workmen.

Bob: My two daughters aren't talking.

Barry: Oh dear, have they fallen out?

Bob: No, they're six months old.

Reincarnation changed my life!

How do you get rid of an alien? Give them their Martian orders.

A pilot has broken the world record for doing the most consecutive loop-the-loops, starting from Hampshire and ending up in Kent. He went over Andover and Dover.

How does Mario communicate with the dead? With a Luigi board.

I love gardening, it's my passion. You dig?

I wish my friend wouldn't show off about all the raffles he's won. It's not a competition.

Bob: Phone your wife and ask her to meet us in a prominent part of the shopping centre.
Barry: Escalator?
Bob: No, ask her now.

Superman goes into a supermarket to buy some groceries. He pays for them at the checkout and the assistant says, 'Do you need a bag?' Superman says, 'No thanks, I'm saving the planet.'

I'm thinking of opening a shop selling protein supplements called Buy the Whey.

Ever since moving to Taiwan's capital, I've become more outgoing and competitive. I have a Taipei personality.

My wife and I first met at a coconut shy. We hit it off immediately.

My cat pretends not to like milk, but when it's there she just laps it up.

Why is Harrison Ford good at touching his toes? Because he can get his hands so low.

Why don't sheep wear knee pads when they skate? Because they like to graze.

My friend doesn't like to talk about his recent

elbow operation. It's a sore point.

My wife asked me to change a plug so I refused.

My brother just moved in next door. We're very close.

Bob: How do you do?
Barry: How do I do what?

When I was on holiday in Hong Kong, a passer-by consoled me after I had my Chinese dictionary stolen. I didn't know how to thank her.

My friend's dieting at the moment, so I bought

her some electronic cutlery that monitors each mouthful. It's the fork that counts.

What trousers does a coffee enthusiast wear? Kappa chinos.

Bob: My daughters are getting their hair dyed blonde tomorrow.
Barry: Platinum?
Bob: No, they don't like pigtails.

What did Emilio Estevez, Molly Ringwald and Rob Lowe buy from Ikea? Brat pack furniture.

My friend lost his job as a banker and now busks for a living. It's all change for him at the moment.

How do trees shed their leaves each year? It happens autumnatically.

On my daughter's first day of school I told my son to keep his sister company. He said, 'I'm six years old, I don't have a sister company.'

I was furious when I spilt my energy drink and saw what the barman was using to mop it up. It was like a rag to a Red Bull.

I work on the assembly line for a robotic waiter manufacturer. It puts food on the table.

Why did the Queen say yes when the Beefeater asked her out? She didn't want to let her guard down.

I found one of last year's conkers under the sofa. Ah, that old chestnut!

Bob: I had an out-of-body experience last week.
Barry: Blimey, that must have been terrifying.
Bob: Yes, I was beside myself.

When I was little, I tried smoking a cigarette. I wanted to look cool in front of my friends, but I blew it.

What do you get if you cross *Dracula* with *Star Wars*? Nosferatu-D2.

Someone's stolen my steroids. Give me strength!

Bob: How are you feeling after you lost a finger in that accident?
Barry: Well, I'm not 100%.

I've lost loads of weight since I started using a George Foreman grill. The fat just falls off.

How did the farmer bring down a spaceship? He used his tractor beam.

I used to think everyone was indecisive, but then a certain person proved me wrong.

I tried to quit smoking by going to Istanbul in winter. It's true what they say – cold Turkey is horrible!

Boarder collie

THE END

THANK YOU!

Thank you for reading this book. I really hope you enjoyed it!

For the latest news on the author please visit jokebooks.co.uk or follow @nickjonezy on Twitter.

By the same author:

Gagged and Bound – A book of puns, one-liners and dad jokes

Gagged and Bound 2 – More puns, one-liners and dad jokes

'It's what it says on the tin: a succession of one-liners, puns and dad jokes going at your laughing muscles in a joyously pell-mell, headlong way. It's irresistible.' **The Bookbag**

'This is a very funny book.' **Red City Review**

'I would recommend this book to anyone looking for a joke book that's varied and full of easy one-liners.' **Reader's Favorite**

Available in paperback and digital formats on Amazon and other websites.

Printed in Great Britain
by Amazon